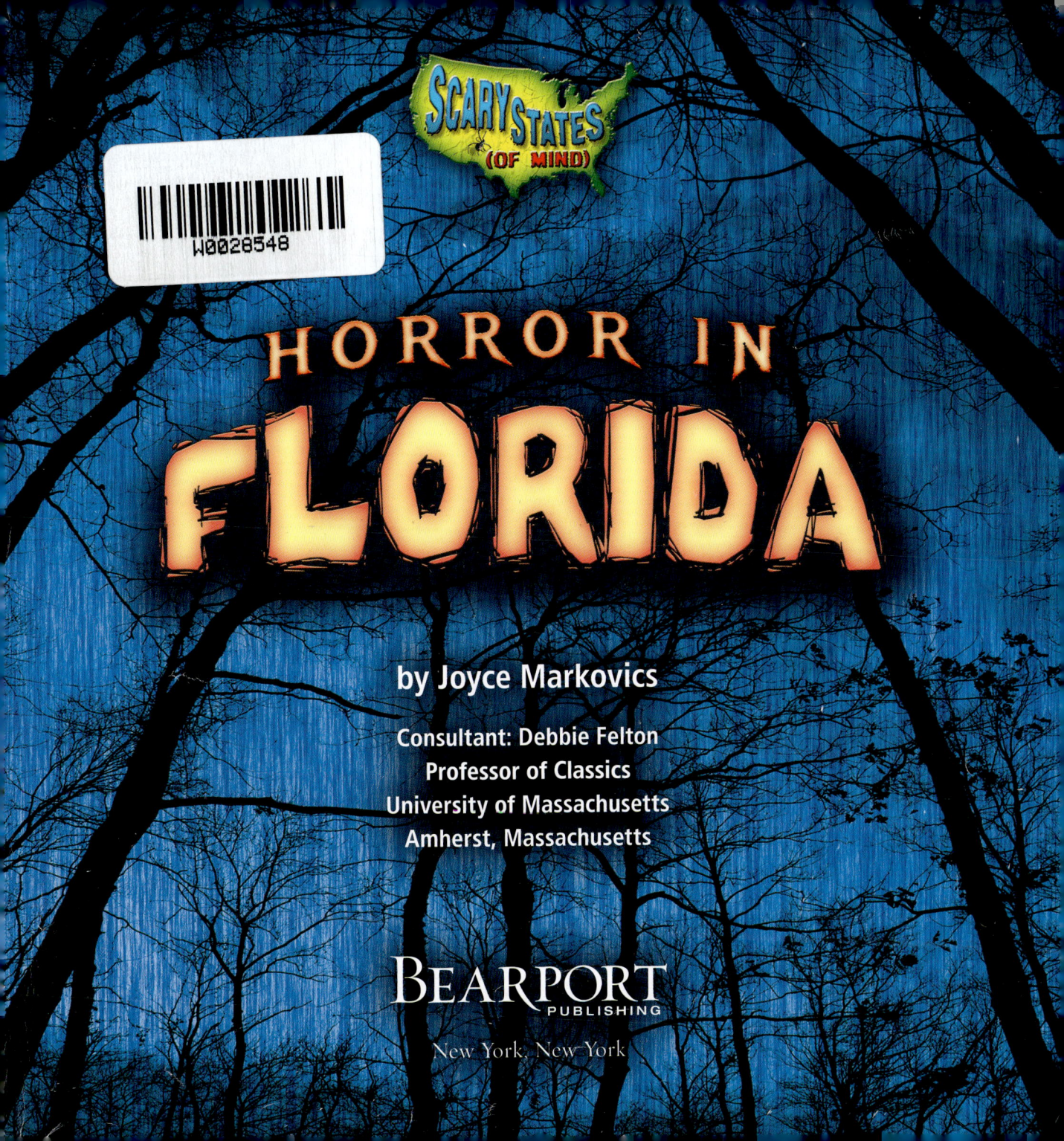

Scary States (of Mind)

HORROR IN FLORIDA

by Joyce Markovics

Consultant: Debbie Felton
Professor of Classics
University of Massachusetts
Amherst, Massachusetts

BEARPORT PUBLISHING

New York, New York

Credits

Cover, © FloridaStock/Shutterstock, © Robert Ranson/Shutterstock, © Khomenko Maryna/Shutterstock, and © Svet_Feo/Shutterstock; TOC, © Rudy Umans/Shutterstock; 4–5, © Khomenko Maryna/Shutterstock, © Robert Ranson/Shutterstock, and © FloridaStock/Shutterstock; 6, © Lloyd Smith/Shutterstock; 7, © Mary Terriberry/Shutterstock; 8–9, © Shimon Bar/Shutterstock and © Vintage Images/Alamy; 10, © Susan Smith/CC BY-NC-ND 2.0; 11, © M. Timothy O'Keefe/Alamy; 13, © Cayobo/CC BY 2.0; 14L, © waewkid/iStock; 14–15, © Allison Michael/Shutterstock; 16, © Ihor Martsenyuk/Shutterstock and © Zacarias Pereira da Mata/Shutterstock; 17, © Chayut Kulsiripipat/Shutterstock; 18, © Lario Tus/Shutterstock; 19, © fisherbray; 20L, © Paradise Studio/Shutterstock; 20–21, © jaimie tuchman/Shutterstock; 23, © Kurit afshen/Shutterstock.

Publisher: Kenn Goin
Senior Editor: Joyce Tavolacci
Creative Director: Spencer Brinker
Photo Researcher: Thomas Persano
Cover: Kim Jones

Library of Congress Cataloging-in-Publication Data in process at time of publication (2020)
Library of Congress Control Number: 2019007180
ISBN-13: 978-1-64280-511-6

Copyright © 2020 Bearport Publishing Company, Inc. All rights reserved. No part of this publication may be reproduced in whole or in part, stored in any retrieval system, or transmitted in any form or by any means, electronic, mechanical, photocopying, recording, or otherwise, without written permission from the publisher.

For more information, write to Bearport Publishing Company, Inc., 45 West 21st Street, Suite 3B, New York, New York 10010. Printed in the United States of America.

10 9 8 7 6 5 4 3 2 1

Contents

Horror in Florida 4

The Haunted Lighthouse 6

Demon Doll 10

The Lake of Skulls 14

Ghost Bridge 18

Spooky Spots in Florida 22
Glossary 23
Index 24
Read More 24
Learn More Online 24
About the Author 24

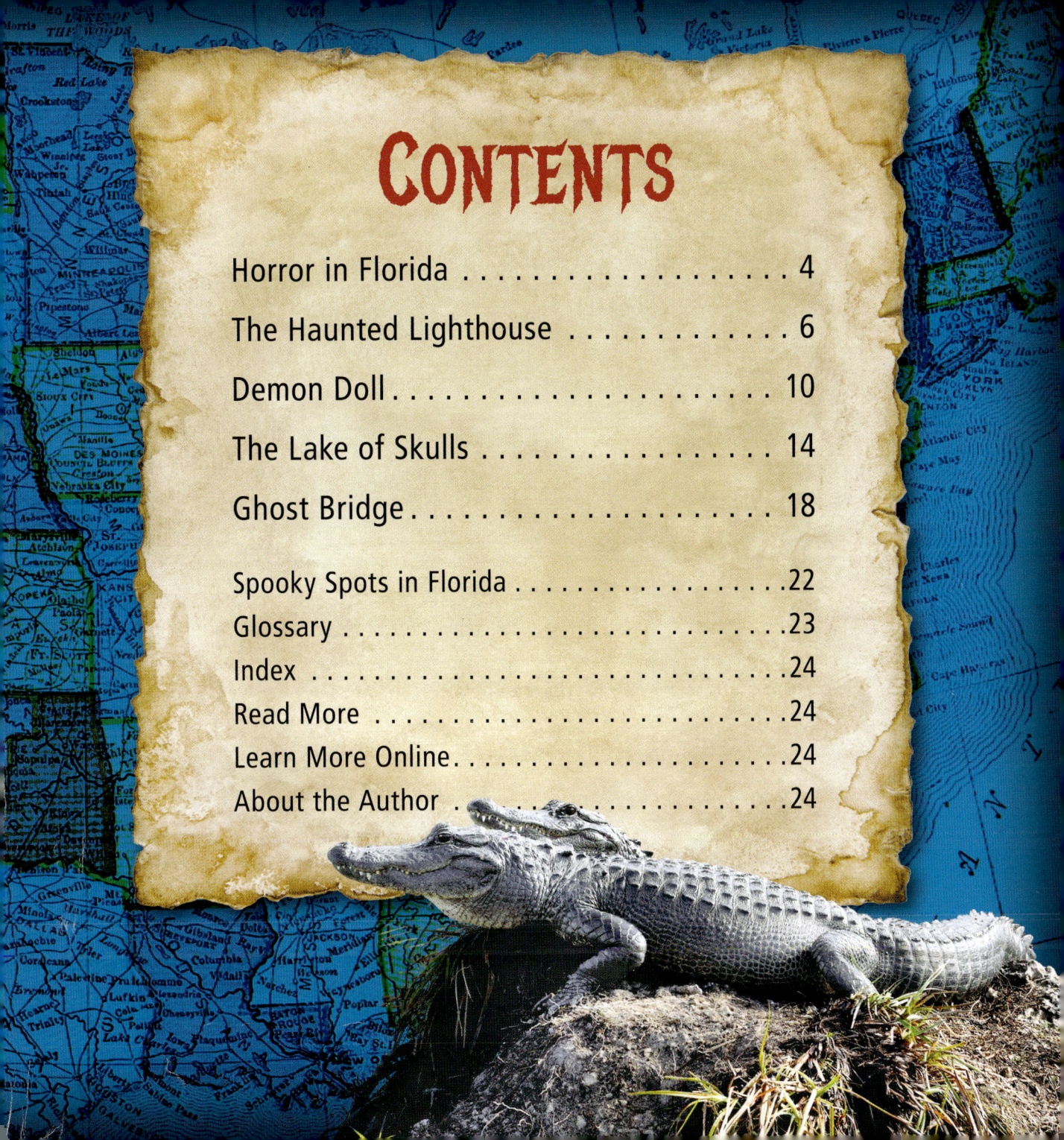

Horror in Florida

There's a dark side to Florida. Beyond the sunny skies is a deeply spooky world. Strange creatures **lurk** in swamps. Ghosts **slink** in the shadows. Be careful where you go—especially on a stormy night.

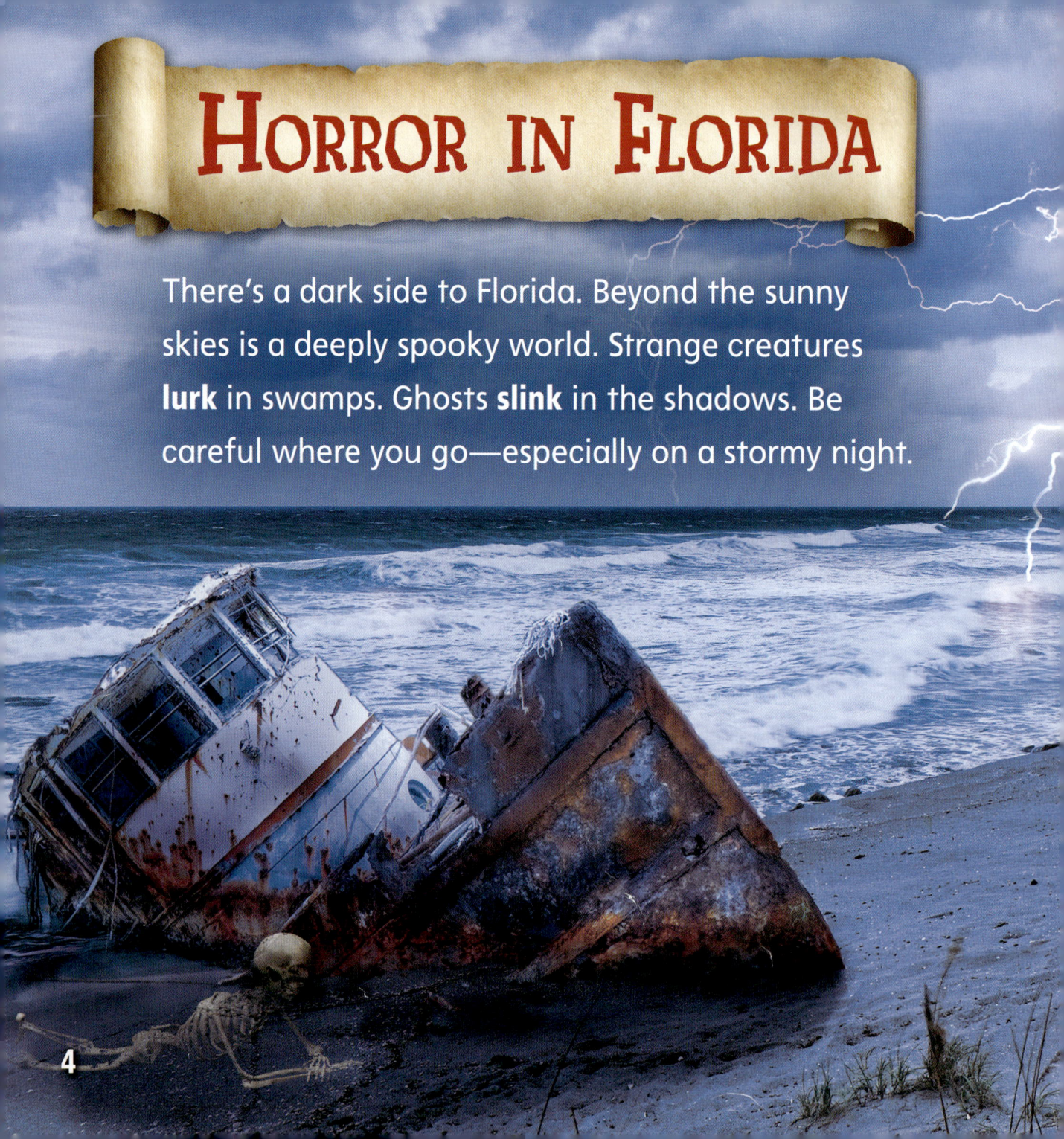

Get ready to read four terrifying tales about Florida. Turn the page . . . if you dare.

The Haunted Lighthouse

St. Augustine Lighthouse, St. Augustine

An old **lighthouse** rises 165 feet (50 m) above the Atlantic Ocean. For over a hundred years, the tower has guided ships at sea. It may also serve as a **beacon** for ghosts.

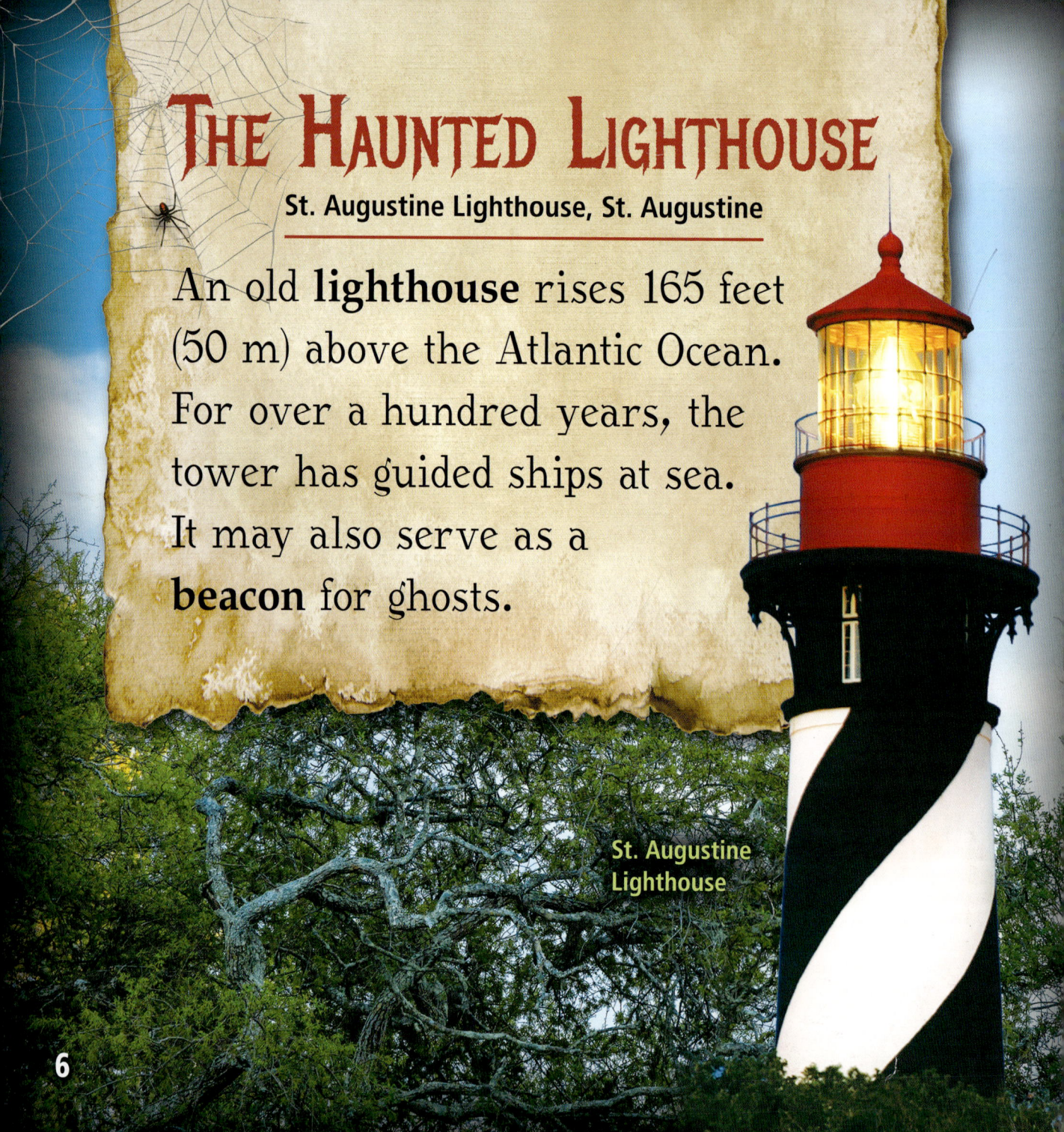

St. Augustine Lighthouse

In the 1850s, Joseph Andreu was the **keeper** of the St. Augustine Lighthouse. In December 1859, he was painting the tower when the **scaffold** he was standing on gave way. Joseph crashed to the ground with a thud. He died minutes later.

In recent times, visitors have spotted a ghostly man at the top of the lighthouse. Could it be Joseph Andreu?

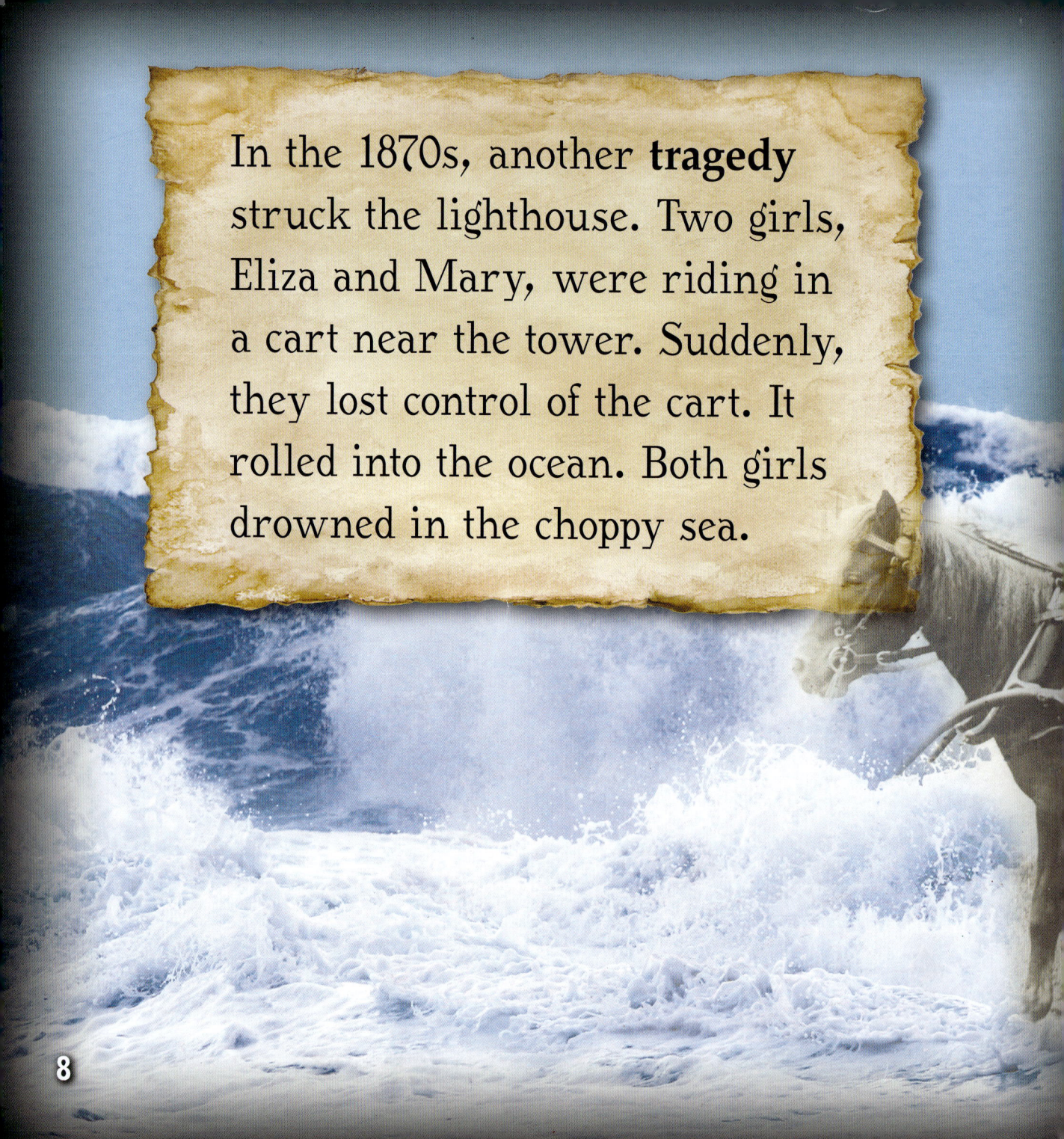

In the 1870s, another **tragedy** struck the lighthouse. Two girls, Eliza and Mary, were riding in a cart near the tower. Suddenly, they lost control of the cart. It rolled into the ocean. Both girls drowned in the choppy sea.

Often at night as waves crash, visitors report hearing the laughter of two girls. Sometimes, a figure appears, wearing the blue dress that Mary had on when she died.

Demon Doll

Fort East Martello Museum, Key West

When Florida artist Gene Otto was a boy, his family gave him a lifelike doll. The large doll, called Robert, was dressed in a little sailor suit. Gene spoke to the doll and took it everywhere. When something bad happened, Gene would say, "I didn't do it. Robert did it."

Robert the doll

Robert the doll is kept at the Fort East Martello Museum, where Gene Otto once worked.

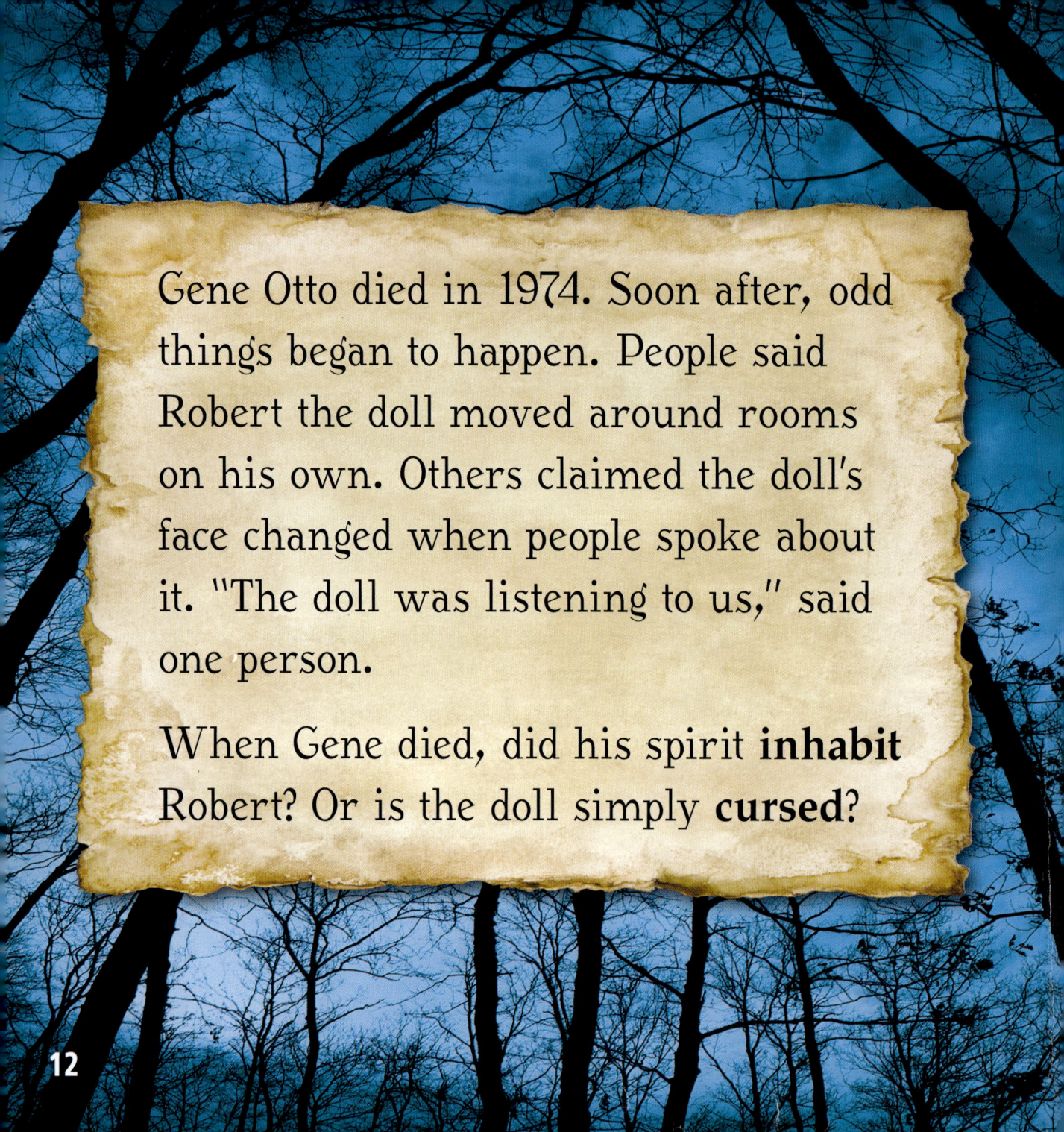

Gene Otto died in 1974. Soon after, odd things began to happen. People said Robert the doll moved around rooms on his own. Others claimed the doll's face changed when people spoke about it. "The doll was listening to us," said one person.

When Gene died, did his spirit **inhabit** Robert? Or is the doll simply **cursed**?

Robert the doll has also been blamed for causing phones and cameras to not work.

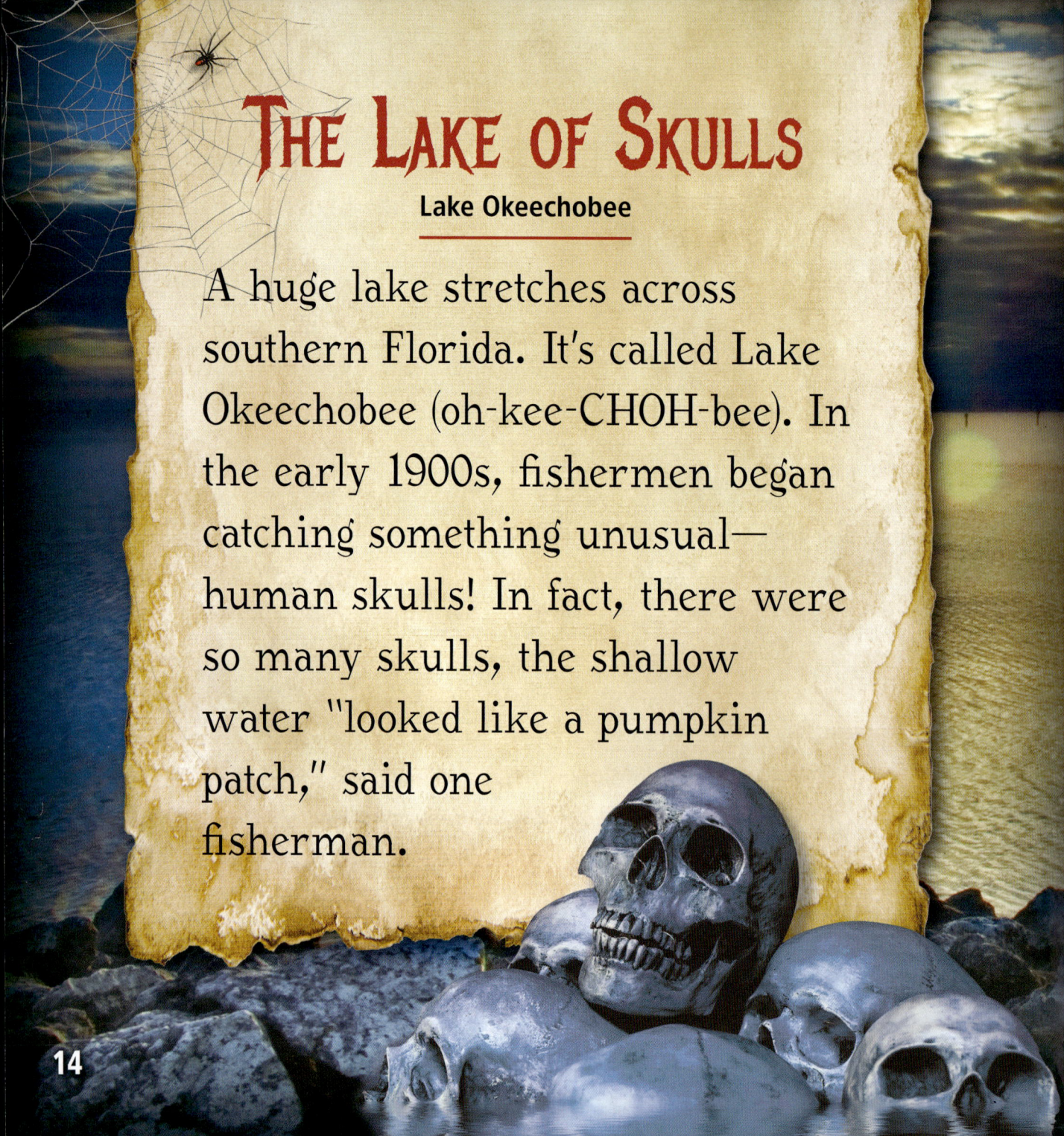

The Lake of Skulls

Lake Okeechobee

A huge lake stretches across southern Florida. It's called Lake Okeechobee (oh-kee-CHOH-bee). In the early 1900s, fishermen began catching something unusual—human skulls! In fact, there were so many skulls, the shallow water "looked like a pumpkin patch," said one fisherman.

Lake Okeechobee

Near where the skulls were found, a person uncovered 50 human **skeletons!** Where had all the bones come from? No one knows.

Every year, people report seeing shadowy bodies floating just above the water. Have the dead risen to tell their stories?

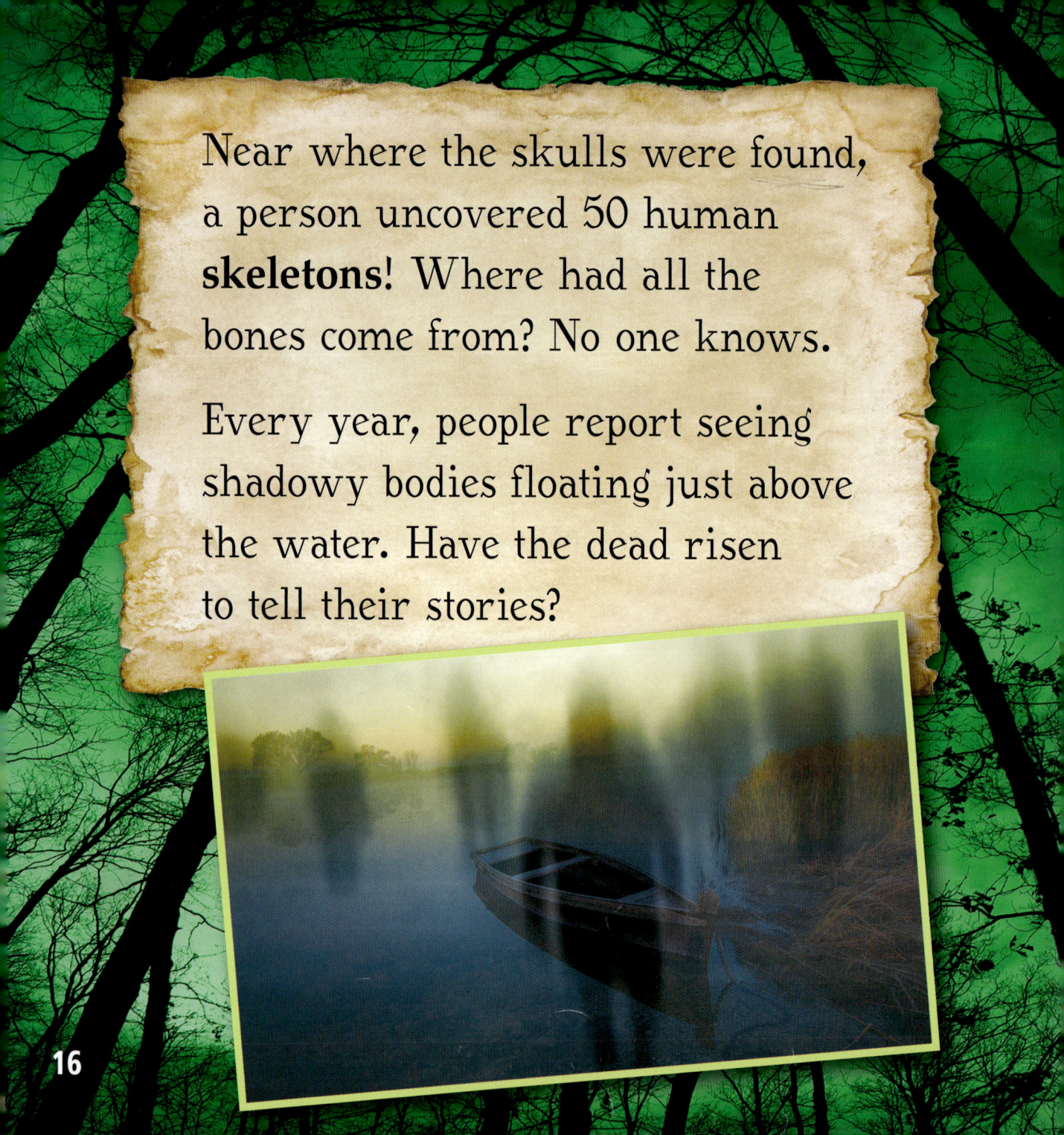

Some of the bones are over 1,000 years old!

17

GHOST BRIDGE
Bellamy Bridge, Marianna

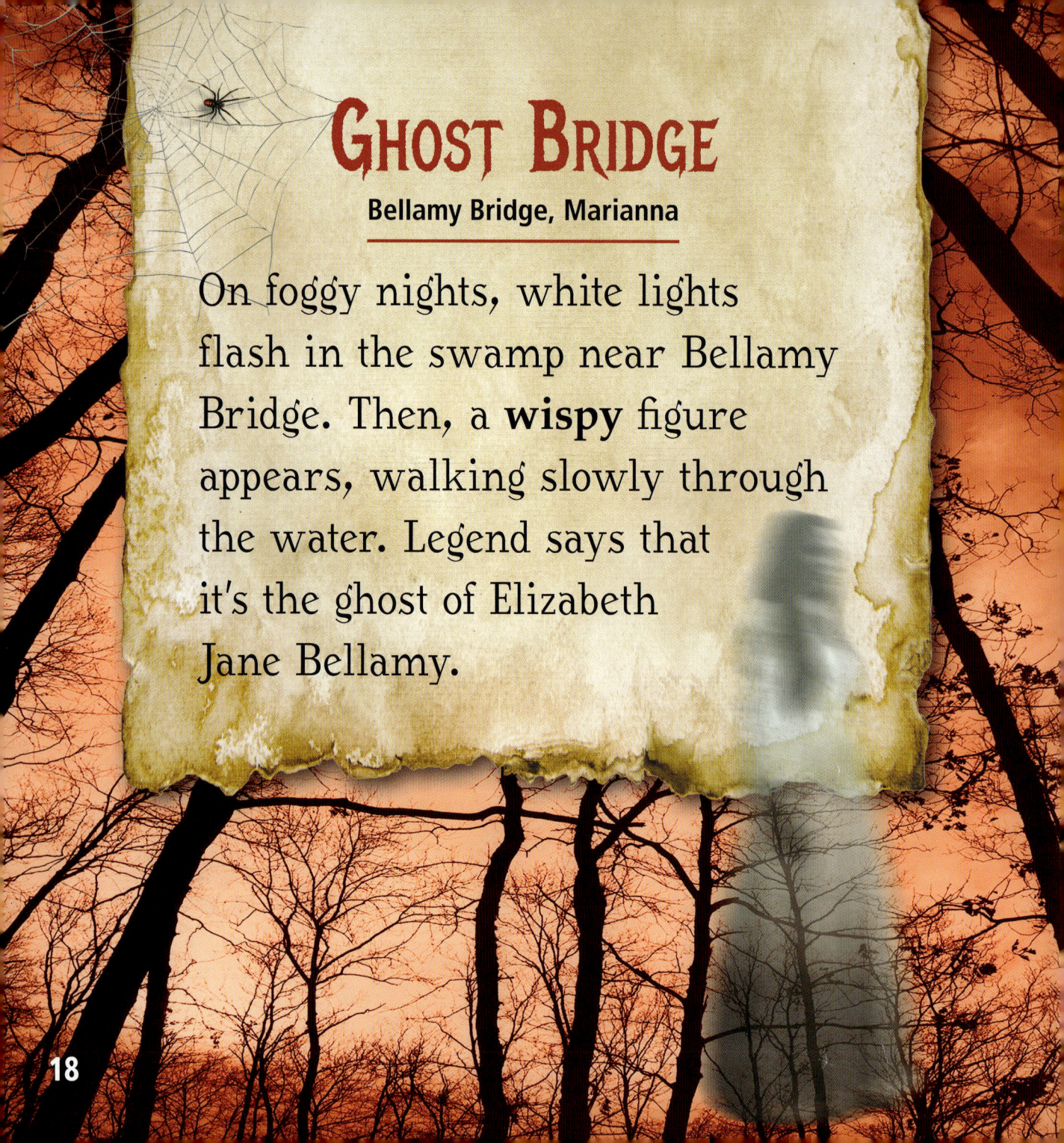

On foggy nights, white lights flash in the swamp near Bellamy Bridge. Then, a **wispy** figure appears, walking slowly through the water. Legend says that it's the ghost of Elizabeth Jane Bellamy.

The Bellamy Bridge was built in 1914.

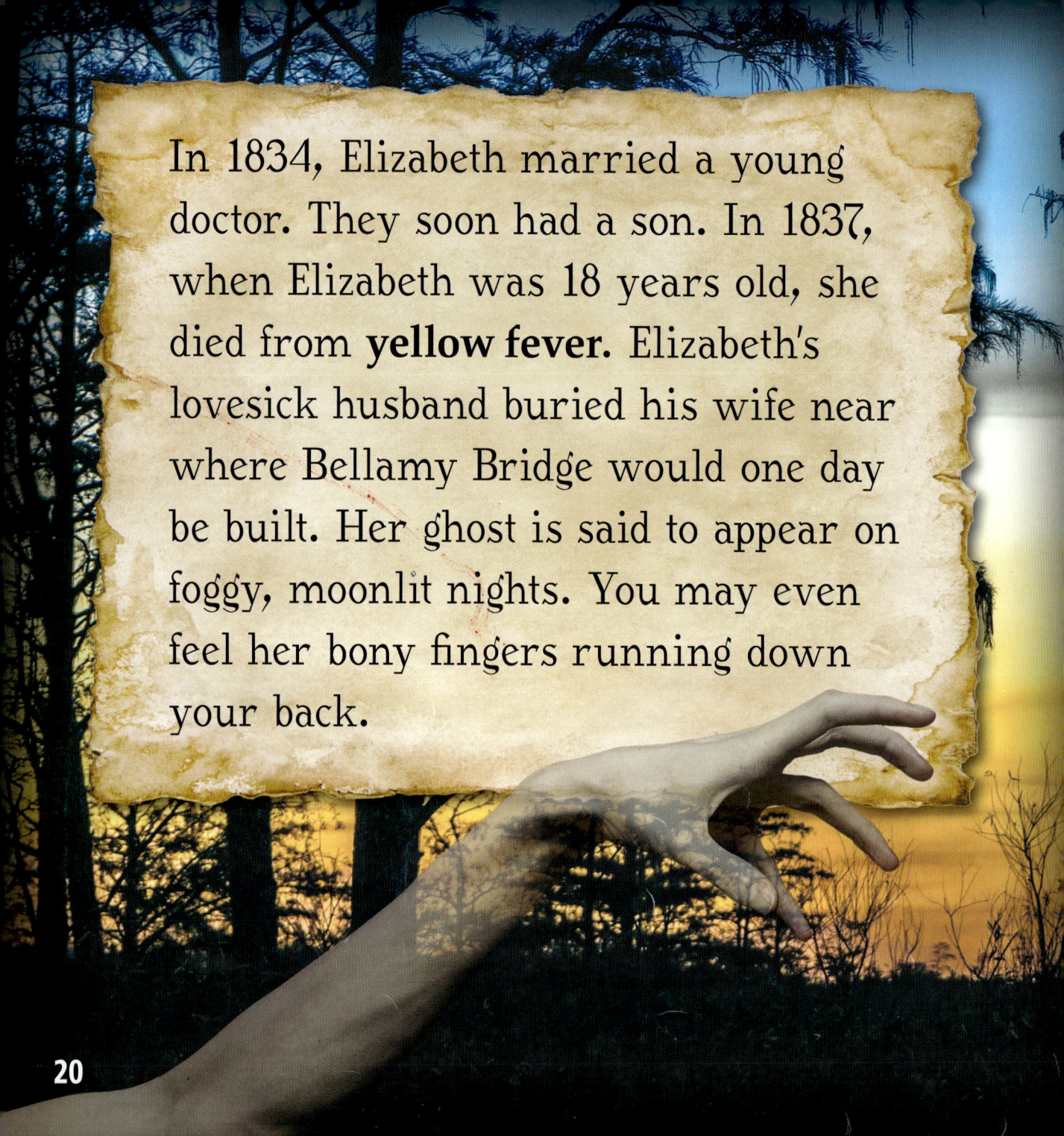

In 1834, Elizabeth married a young doctor. They soon had a son. In 1837, when Elizabeth was 18 years old, she died from **yellow fever.** Elizabeth's lovesick husband buried his wife near where Bellamy Bridge would one day be built. Her ghost is said to appear on foggy, moonlit nights. You may even feel her bony fingers running down your back.

Spooky Spots in Florida

Bellamy Bridge
Visit a bridge haunted by a young mother.

St. Augustine Lighthouse
Explore a lighthouse that has a deathly glow.

Lake Okeechobee
Check out a lake that's also a grave!

Fort East Martello Museum
Learn about Robert the demonic doll.

ALABAMA
GEORGIA
Atlantic Ocean
Gulf of Mexico
FLORIDA
Lake Okeechobee

CANADA
UNITED STATES
MEXICO

22

Glossary

beacon (BEE-kuhn) a light or other object that can serve as a signal or guide

cursed (KURST) bringing unhappiness or bad luck

inhabit (in-HAB-it) to live in or occupy a place

keeper (KEE-per) a person who guards or looks after something, such as a lighthouse

lighthouse (LITE-hous) a tower with a light that guides ships away from shore at night or during heavy fog

lurk (LURK) to secretly hide

scaffold (SKAF-uhld) a raised platform made of wooden planks

skeletons (SKEL-ih-tunz) the bones of humans or other animals

slink (SLINK) to move in a smooth, quiet way

tragedy (TRAJ-uh-dee) a sad and terrible event

wispy (WIS-pee) fine or thin

yellow fever (YEL-oh FEE-vur) a deadly disease spread by mosquitoes

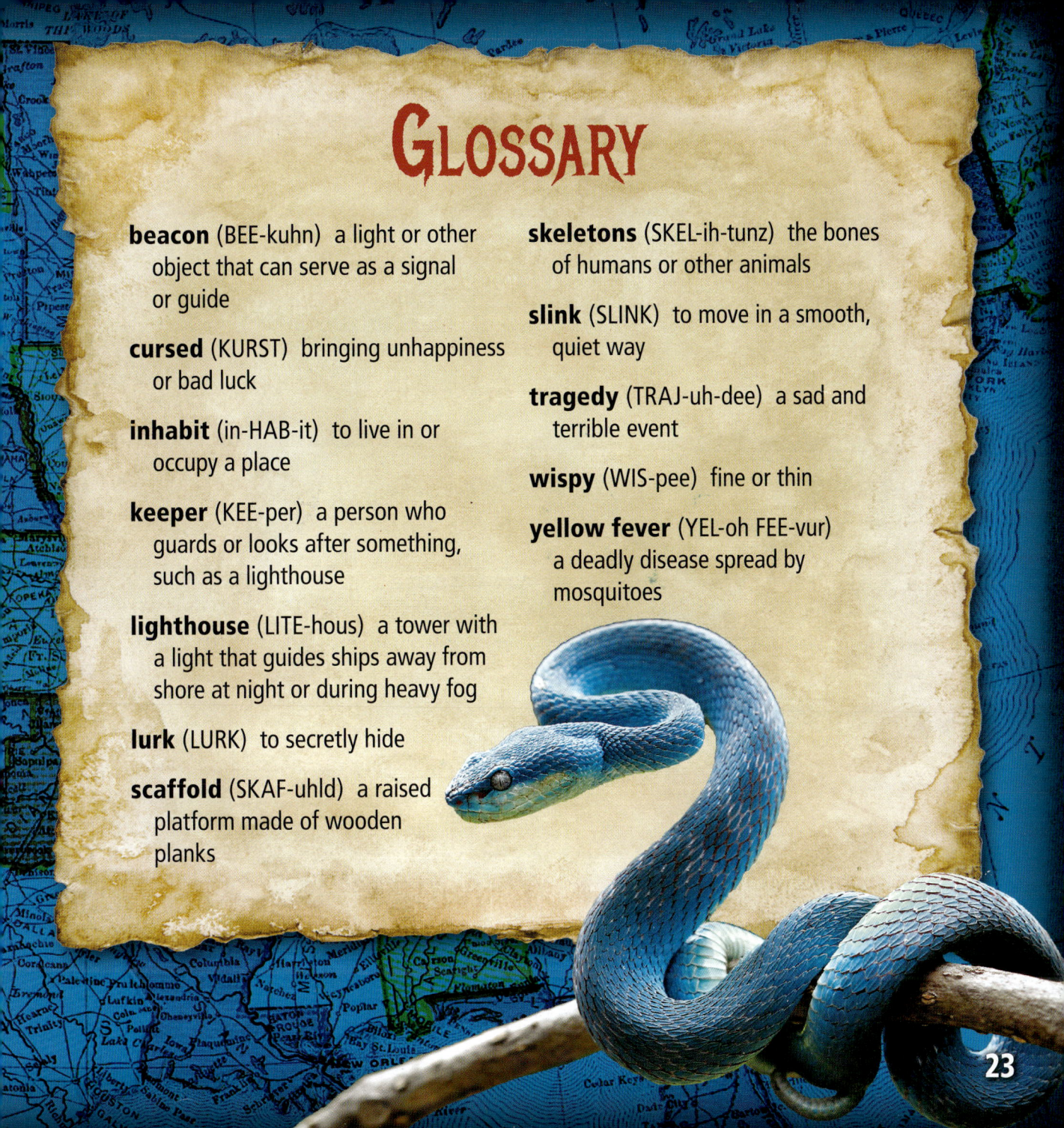

23

Index

Andreu, Joseph 7
Bellamy Bridge 18–19, 20–21, 22
Fort East Martello Museum 10–11, 12–13, 22
Key West, Florida 10
Lake Okeechobee, Florida 14–15, 16–17, 22
Marianna, Florida 18, 20–21
Otto, Gene 10–11, 12–13
Robert the doll 10–11, 12–13
St. Augustine, Florida 6–7
St. Augustine Lighthouse 6–7, 8–9, 22
yellow fever 20

Read More

Markovics, Joyce. *Chilling Cemeteries (Tiptoe Into Scary Places).* New York: Bearport (2017).

Phillips, Dee. *Nightmare in the Hidden Morgue (Cold Whispers II).* New York: Bearport (2017).

Learn More Online

To learn more about the horror in Florida, visit:
www.bearportpublishing.com/ScaryStates

About the Author

Joyce Markovics is an author who lives in a 160-year-old house. She recently found a small pet cemetery in her backyard. She sometimes places flowers on the tiny graves.